Our Wound is Not So Recent

Our Wound is Not So Recent

Thinking the Paris Killings of 13 November

Alain Badiou

Translated by Robin Mackay

polity

First published in French as *Notre mal vient de plus loin. Penser les tueries du 13 novembre,* © Librairie Arthème Fayard, 2016

This English edition © Polity Press, 2016

Polity Press
65 Bridge Street
Cambridge CB2 1UR, UK

Polity Press
350 Main Street
Malden, MA 02148, USA

ISBN-13: 978-1-5095-1493-9

A catalogue record for this book is available from the British Library.

Library of Congress Cataloging-in-Publication Data

Names: Badiou, Alain, author.
Title: Our wound is not so recent : thinking the Paris killings of 13 November / Alain Badiou.
Other titles: Notre mal vient de plus loin. English
Description: Malden, MA : Polity Press, 2016. | Includes bibliographical references.
Identifiers: LCCN 2016013510| ISBN 9781509514939 (hardback : alk. paper) | ISBN 9781509514953 (mobi)
Subjects: LCSH: Terrorism--France--Paris--History--21st century. | Terrorism--Social aspects. | Political violence. | Capitalism.
Classification: LCC HV6433.F7 B3313 2016 | DDC 363.3250944/361090512--dc23
LC record available at https://lccn.loc.gov/2016013510

Typeset in 12.5 on 15pt Adobe Garamond by
Servis Filmsetting Ltd, Stockport, Cheshire
Printed and bound in the UK by Clays Ltd, St Ives PLC

For further information on Polity, visit our website:
politybooks.com

This text is a transcript of a special seminar given by Alain Badiou on 23 November 2015 at the Théâtre de la Commune d'Aubervilliers, Paris. Our thanks to director Marie-José Malis and to the staff of the theatre, for hosting the event.

This evening I would like to talk about what happened on Friday 13 November: what happened to us, what happened to this city, to this country, and ultimately to this world.

I would first like to say in what state of mind I think we should speak of what is an atrocious tragedy. Because, obviously, as we know, and as is being dangerously hammered home by the press and by the authorities, the function of affect, of sensible reaction, is inevitable in this kind of situation, and in a certain sense indispensable. There is something like a trauma, the feeling of an intolerable exception to the regime of ordinary life, an unbearable irruption of death. This is something we all feel, and which we can neither contain nor subject to criticism.

But all the same, we need to realize – and this is the starting point for considering what I call our 'state of mind' – that this inevitable affect, in these kinds of tragic circumstances, exposes us to many risks, risks that I would like to enumerate, so as to indicate what my method here will be.

I see three principal risks to which we are exposed, following this drama, by the unadulterated domination of trauma and affect.

The first is that of authorizing the state to take futile and unacceptable measures, measures that in reality function only for its own profit. The state is abruptly brought to the fore and for a moment rediscovers, or thinks it has rediscovered, its function of symbolic representation, as the guarantor of the unity of the nation, and other such postures. Which allows us – and I'll come back to this – to perceive in the senior staff a rather sinister but undeniable enjoyment of this criminal situation. In such conditions, we must nonetheless maintain a certain measured attitude. We must remain capable of discriminating, in what is done, in what is pronounced, between that which is inevitable and necessary, and that which is futile and unacceptable. This is the first precaution I think is necessary: that of remaining measured in regard to – let me say once again – the both inevitable and indispensable nature of affect.

The second risk of this domination of the

sensible, let's call it that, is the reinforcing of identitarian drives. This, also, is a natural mechanism.
It is obvious that, when a family member dies in
an accident, the family gathers, pulls together and,
in a certain sense, consolidates. In the days following this tragedy we have been assured, indeed
they tell us again and again, with the tricolour
flag in hand, that a horrific massacre on French
territory can only reinforce national sentiment.
As if trauma automatically referred us back to an
identity. Hence the words 'French' and 'France'
are heard from every quarter, as if they were a
self-evident component of the situation. Well,
let's ask the question: How so? What actually is
'France' in this affair? What do we mean today
when we speak of 'France' and of the 'French'?
In reality, these are very complex questions. We
absolutely must not lose sight of this complex-
ity: the words 'France', 'French', today have no
simple, self-evident meaning. Moreover, I think
that we must make the effort, precisely against
this identitarian drive which would incorporate
the terrible event into a sort of false pretext, to
remind ourselves that such terrifying mass murders have happened and are still happening every
day elsewhere in the world. Yes, every day, in

Nigeria and Mali, very recently indeed, in Iraq, in Pakistan, in Syria. . . . It's important also to remember that in October 2015, two hundred Russians were massacred in a sabotaged aeroplane, and that in France, emotions didn't run particularly high about it. Perhaps the supposed 'French' identify all Russians with the wicked Putin!

I think that it is one of the fundamental tasks of justice always to broaden, as far as possible, the space of public affects, to struggle against their identitarian restriction, to remember and to know that the space of misfortune is a space that we must envisage, ultimately, on the scale of all of humanity, and that we must never retreat into declarations that limit it to some identity or other. Otherwise, misfortune itself ends up confirming the notion that what counts are identities. Now, the idea that what counts in a misfortune is only the identity of the victims is a perilous perception of the tragic event itself, because inevitably, *this idea transforms justice into vengeance.*

Obviously, the temptation to vengeance, with this type of mass criminal act, is a drive that seems natural. The proof of this is that, in our country, which always boasts of its rule of law, and which rejects the death penalty, the police, in the type of circumstance that we have seen here, kill the murderers as soon as they find them, without – make no mistake – without any kind of trial; and that no one, it seems, is bothered by this. However we must remember that vengeance, far from being an act of justice, always opens up a cycle of atrocities. Long ago, the great Greek tragedies opposed the logic of justice to the logic of vengeance. The universality of justice is the contrary of familial, provincial, national, identitarian vengeance. This is the fundamental subject of Aeschylus' *Oresteia*. The identitarian reaction to tragedy opens up the danger of conceiving the search for the murderers as a quest for vengeance pure and simple: 'We will kill those who killed.' There may well be a certain inevitability in the desire to kill those who have killed. But there is certainly nothing to celebrate in it, nothing to proclaim and trumpet as if it were a victory of thought, of spirit, of civilization, or of justice. Vengeance is primitive, abject, and, moreover, dangerous – the Greeks taught us this a long time ago.

From this point of view, I would also like to voice my disquiet about things that have been hailed as self-evident. For example: Obama's declaration.[1] It didn't amount to much, this declaration. It came down to saying that this terrible crime was not only a crime against France, a crime against Paris, but a crime against humanity. Very good, quite right. But President Obama doesn't make such a declaration every time there is a mass murder of this kind: he doesn't do so when such things take place far away, in an Iraq become incomprehensible, in a hazy Pakistan, in a fanatical Nigeria, or in a Congo that is at the heart of darkness. So the statement contains the idea, a supposedly self-evident idea, that this wounded humanity lives in France, and doubtless also in the United States, rather than in Nigeria or in India, in Iraq, in Pakistan, or in the Congo.

In truth, Obama wanted to remind us that, for him, humanity can above all be identified with our good old West. And that one can therefore say: humanity equals the West – we hear this, like a *basso continuo*, in many declarations, in official statements and news stories alike. One of the forms taken by this unacceptable identitarian

[1] 'We are reminded in this time of tragedy that the bonds of liberté and égalité and fraternité are not only values that the French people care so deeply about, but they are values that we share.'

6

presumption, and I will come back to this, is the opposition between barbarians and the civilized. Now, it is scandalous, from the point of view of the most elementary justice, to let it be understood, even if not deliberately, even indirectly, that some parts of humanity are more human than others; and I'm afraid that, in this affair, that has been done and continues to be done.

I think we need to break the habit that is very much present – including the way in which things are told, presented, arranged, or on the contrary are killed, redacted – yes, we must lose the habit, almost embedded in the unconscious itself, of thinking that a death in the West is terrible but that a thousand deaths in Africa, in Asia, or in the Middle East, or even in Russia, are ultimately no big deal. This is of course the heritage of colonial imperialism, the heritage of what we call the West – that is, the advanced, civilized, democratic countries: the habit of seeing oneself as representative of all humanity and of human civilization as such. This is the second danger that lies in wait for us if we react on the basis of affect alone.

And then there is a third danger, that of doing exactly what the murderers want – namely, to obtain a disproportionate effect, to be constantly visible with their anarchic and violent actions, and ultimately to create in the entourage of the victims a passion such that, in the end, one will no longer be able to distinguish between those who initiated the crime and those who suffered it. Because the aim of this kind of carnage, this kind of abject violence, is to arouse in the victims, in their families, their neighbours, their compatriots, a sort of obscure subject, I'll call it that, an obscure subject at once depressed and vengeful, a subject constituted by the nature of the crime as a violent and almost inexplicable strike; but one that is also homogeneous with the strategy of its sponsors. This strategy anticipates the effects of the obscure subject: all reason will be lost, including political reason, affect will take the upper hand, and in this way one will spread everywhere the couplet of dejected depression ('I'm stunned', 'I'm shocked') and the spirit of vengeance, a couplet that will leave the state and the official avengers free to do anything whatsoever. Thus, in accordance with the desires of the criminals, this obscure subject will reveal that it too is capable of the worst acts, and in the end will have to be recognized by all as symmetrical with those who organized the crime.

So, to counter these three risks, I think that we must manage to *think* what has happened. Let's set out from the following principle: *nothing that anyone does is unintelligible*. To say 'I don't understand', 'I'll never understand', 'I can't understand', is always a defeat. We can't leave anything in the register of the unthinkable. It is the vocation of thought, if we want to be able, among other things, to oppose that which we declare unthinkable, to think it. Of course there are absolutely irrational, criminal, pathological behaviours, but all of these constitute objects of thought like any others, and do not leave thought lost or unable to take stock of them. The declaration of the unthinkable is always a defeat of thought, and the defeat of thought is always precisely the victory of irrational and criminal behaviours.

So I will try to give you a comprehensive elucidation of what has happened. I will in a certain sense treat this mass murder as one of a number of current symptoms of a grave malady of the contemporary world, of this world as a whole, and I will try to indicate what would be necessary, and what paths could be taken, for a long-term recovery from the sickness of which the proliferation of these kinds of events in the world is a particularly violent and spectacular symptom.

This aim of giving a comprehensive elucidation will govern the sequence of my exposition, its logic.

First of all I will try to go from the situation of the whole world as I see it, as I believe it can be thought synthetically, to the mass murders and to the war that has been declared or pronounced by the state. And then I will track back from there in the other direction, towards the overall situation, no longer as it is, but as we must desire it to become, as we must will and act in order that such symptoms might be banished.

In a first stage, then, we'll move from the general situation of the world to the event with which we are concerned; and then we'll go back from the event to the world situation in a clarified form. This there-and-back movement should allow us to indicate certain necessities and tasks.

It will comprise seven successive parts. So it will take a while!

The first part will present the objective structure of the contemporary world, the general framework of what is happening: what has happened here, but is happening elsewhere almost every day. That is, the objective structure of the contemporary world as it was established, beginning in the 1980s. What is the state of our world, from the point of view of what has been put into place – at first insidiously, then quite overtly, and then with ruthless determination – over the last thirty years or so?

Secondly, I will examine the principal effects of this structure of the contemporary world upon populations, their diversity, their interactions, and their subjectivities.

This will prepare the way for my third point, which concerns the typical subjectivities created by this process. For I believe that this world has created singular types of subjectivity that are characteristic of the period. As you will see, I distinguish between three typical subjectivities.

The fourth part, which will bring me close to the primary object of this exposition, will bear upon what I would call the contemporary figures of fascism. As you will see, I think that the perpetrators of what happened in Paris do deserve to be called fascists, in a renewed, contemporary sense of the term.

Once we reach this point, then I will try to go back in the other direction, towards what we must do to change the world, in order to exclude such criminal symptoms. The fifth part will therefore be dedicated to the event itself, in its different component parts. Who are the killers? Who are the agents of this mass murder? And how can we describe what they did?

In sixth place, we will have the state's reaction and the shaping of public opinion around the two words 'France' and 'war'.

The seventh part will be entirely dedicated to the attempt to construct a different thought, that is to say to subtract ourselves from this moulding of public opinion and from the reactive orientation of the state. It will bear upon the conditions, clarified by this entire trajectory, of what I would call a return to politics, in the sense of a return to the politics of emancipation, or the return of a politics that refuses all inclusion in the schema of the world from which I set out.

I

Structure of the Contemporary World

I want to talk about the structure of the contemporary world as I see it and, of course, in so far as it will help us to clarify what is at stake here. I think that one can describe it, in broad brushstrokes, by way of three themes, themes that are profoundly intertwined, entangled with one another.

Firstly – and this may seem like a crushing banality, but in my view, the consequences of this banality are far from having been drawn: for thirty years now, what we have seen is the triumph of globalized capitalism.

This triumph is first of all, quite visibly, the return of a sort of primitive energy of capitalism, in the form of what is known by the contestable name of neoliberalism, but which is in fact the reappearance and the rediscovered efficacy of what has always been the constitutive ideology of capitalism, namely liberalism. The 'neo' is not necessarily justified. I don't think that what is happening is as 'neo' as all that, when we look at it closely enough. In any case, the triumph of globalized capitalism is a kind of rediscovered energy, the return of an uncontested capacity to display, now quite overtly and, if I might say so, without any shame whatsoever, the general characteristics of this very specific type of organization of production, of exchange, and ultimately of entire societies; and also its claim to be the only reasonable path for the historical destiny of humanity. All of this, which was invented and formulated around the end of the eighteenth century in England, and which subsequently dominated unchallenged for decades, has been rediscovered with a sort of ferocious glee by our masters of today.

When globalized, it takes on a somewhat different inflection. Today we have a capitalism explicitly installed on a planetary scale. Which is what makes globalized capitalism not only a capitalism that has rediscovered its solvent energy but one that, also, has developed it in such a way that right now, we can say that, considered as a global structure, capitalism exercises a practically unchallenged mastery of the whole of the planet.

The second theme is the weakening of states. This is a rather subtle consequence of the first, but one whose identification is wholly pertinent here.

As you will all know, one of the most widely derided themes of Marxism has been that of the withering away of the state. Marxism announced that the reorganization of the state, following the revolutionary destruction of nation-states dominated by capitalism, would ultimately unfold, through a powerful collective communist-type movement, into a society without a state, a society that Marx called one of 'free association'. Well, today we are seeing a wholly pathological phenomenon, namely a capitalist process of the withering away of states. It is a fundamental phenomenon today, even if it is masked by the subsistence of quite substantial concentrations of power in states, something that will probably continue for a lengthy historical period. But in truth, the general logic of globalized capitalism is to have no direct or intrinsic relation to the subsistence of national states, because today it is deployed on a transnational basis. The multinational character of large companies came to light during the 1960s. But since then, these large companies have become transnational monsters of an entirely other nature.

Finally, the third theme is what I would call the new practices of imperialism, the forceful modes of action, if I can put it that way, of the global extension of capitalism, the new figures of imperialism – that is to say, of the conquest of the planet qua basis of capitalism's existence and profit.

1 The Triumph of Globalized Capital

The triumph of globalized capitalism is something self-evident that is clear to everyone. Today, the world market is the absolute benchmark of planetary historicity. At every moment, it is a question of the world market. We know very well that, when the Shanghai exchange wobbles, the whole world becomes anxious, seems terrorized, wonders what's going to happen, and so on. . . .

The aggression that accompanies this extension

of the dominance of the world market as sole reference of planetary historicity is particularly spectacular. Today we are seeing the destruction, everywhere, of all prior attempts to introduce some measure into capital. By which I mean the past compromises, in particular during the post-war period, between the logic of capital and other logics. Other logics such as that of state control, concessions to unions, caution about concentrations of industrial and banking power, logics of partial nationalization, measures for the control of certain excesses of private property, antitrust laws. . . . And also the introduction of measures that extended social rights to the population, such as the possibility of access to healthcare for all, or forms of limitation of the private exercise of liberal professions, and so on.

All of this is being methodically destroyed, even in the countries that were once its paradigms. I don't even mean socialist states, the late socialist countries: France was one of the countries that offered the most examples of this measured spirit. But all of this is being destroyed today with great determination. Obviously, it began with denationalizations, privatizations. The word 'privatization' is wholly aggressive, even if we no longer realize it. It is a word that directly designates the fact that activities designed for the public good must be handed over to private property as such. It is a word of extraordinary aggression, even if it has now become a commonplace. In the same way, and incessantly – whether from the right or the left, there is no difference between them on this point – entire swathes of social legislation are being undone, whether we are talking about labour law, social security, or the education system. . . .

It must be seen that the objective victory of globalized capitalism is a destructive, aggressive practice. It is not merely some kind of reasoned or reasonable expansion of a particular system of production. And one cannot help but be disquieted by the feeble resistance put up against these successive destructions. This resistance is in fact a constant retreat. It is localized, dispersed, very often corporatist, sectorial, and does not seem to be based on any underlying vision. In reality, for thirty years now it has been an uninterrupted retreat.

We have seen the progressive imposition of a dominant representation that prohibits the least measure or restraint being placed on capitalism.

In this sense, we can say that the logic of capital has been liberated. Liberalism is liberated. There you have it. For thirty years now what we have seen happening, as we stand idly by, is the liberation of liberalism. And this liberation takes two forms: globalization – that is to say, the uninterrupted expansion of capitalism to whole territories such as China – and at the same time the extraordinary power of the concentration of capital – that is to say, of the dialectical movement characteristic of capital: it spreads, and in spreading it concentrates. Expansion and concentration are two modalities, absolutely linked to one another, of the protean form of capital.

Concentrations thus proceed at the same time as privatizations and destructions accelerate. You will all have heard, since it has a somewhat spectacular aspect, about the recent merger of Fnac and Darty, two French retail giants. Here we have the fusion of books and refrigeration! Clearly the aim is strictly financial, and is characteristic of a purely capitalist fusion, with no public interest. These concentrations thus progressively create poles of power that are comparable to states, if not more powerful than some states. These are financial concentrations of power, sometimes productive, speculative, always involving a substantial workforce, often with a powerful militia in their service, and they spread everywhere, often by force, always by corruption. These concentrated poles are transnational, even if they have a diagonal relation to states. In regard to these massive transnational powers, state sovereignty cannot at all be taken for granted.

Thus we see that, just like other large firms, the largest French firm, Total, pays no tax in France. So in what does their 'Frenchness' lie? Well, their headquarters are somewhere in Paris, but . . . . The French state, as you can see, does not really have any hold even on concentrated poles of power that proclaim their French nationality. What is in progress is a victory, a vast and ramified victory, of transnational firms over the sovereignty of states.

But there is also a subjective victory that accompanies this objective victory of capitalism. It is the total eradication of the very idea of any other path. And this is of great importance, because it is the affirmation, in a certain sense a strategic one, that another global, systemic orientation for the organization of production and the social is possible, that is practically absent right now.

So that all proposals, including proposals for resistance, propositions to reintroduce some kind of restraint, and so on, are already situated within a defeatist vision of the general tendency. They are not integrated into a strategy for taking back the territory of the Idea. They are just impotent nostalgia for the epoch of social compromises and semi-statist measures for the control of capital.

It is striking to see how the programme of the *Conseil National de la Résistance* has become such a grand nostalgic model for France – the period when, coming out of the Nazi occupation, French capitalists having in many cases collaborated with the occupiers, the alliance between the Gaullists and the Communists imposed important measures of nationalization and social redistribution.

However, the nostalgia for this reformist programme forgets that at the time, firstly, we had just come out of a world war; secondly, the collaborationist bourgeoisie dared not show its face; and thirdly, there was a powerful communist party. None of this exists today. And the nostalgia for the social programme of the CNR is a dream completely disconnected from the spectacular subjective victory of globalized capitalism. The result of this victory is that, over a relatively short time, between 1975 and 2015, the force of the idea that, whatever the difficulties might be, another possibility existed, has been annulled, reduced to almost nothing. And this is an idea that, still in the 1960s and 1970s, was a driving force for millions of political rebels throughout the world.

This idea, whose generic name, since the nineteenth century, has been 'communism', is today so sickly that we are ashamed to even name it. Well, I'm not. But on the whole, it is criminalized. This criminalization may have its reasons: Stalin, and others. But it is not as if the aim pursued by the advocates of capitalist globalization is an ethical aim, as their media hacks would have us believe. Their aim is the eradication, definitive if possible, of the very idea of a global, systemic alternative to capitalism. We have moved from two to one. This is fundamental. It is not the same thing when, on the same question, there are two ideas in conflict, as when there is only one. And this unicity is the key point in regard to the subjective triumph of capitalism.

2 The Weakening of States

Today, states are ultimately just the local managers of this vast global structure. They represent a kind of mediation – an unstable one, moreover – between the general logic I have just described and particular situations defined by countries, coalitions, federations, states . . . on a case-by-case basis. And it is far from being the case that the norm of power is represented by states and by them alone. Of course, there still exist established state poles, states which still have some vigour, large concentrations of power such as the USA and China. But even in these cases, the process is the same one that we have described. These powers do not stand for anything else.

As I have said, large firms have the lead on medium-sized states. What is more, it is striking that the banks themselves have become so important that it is admitted, as an axiom, that they are 'too big to fail' – this is what is often said of the large American banks. Which means that economic macroscopy trumps state capacity. This is what I call the weakening of states. Not only have states largely become what Marx already thought they were, namely 'the delegates of capital power' (but

I'm not sure whether Marx could have imagined the extent to which, from the 1980s on, reality would prove him right); not only are states the delegates of capital power, but there is increasingly a kind of discordance between the scale upon which large firms exist and the scale upon which states exist, which makes the existence of large firms diagonal to that of states. The power of the great industrial, banking, and retail conglomerates coincides neither with the state sphere, nor even with that of coalitions of states. This capitalist power crosses over states as if it were at once independent of them and mistress of them.

This brings me to my third point – the new practices of imperialism.

3 The New Practices of Imperialism

As you know, the old imperialism, that of the nineteenth century, was entirely governed by the idea of the nation, the nation-state. Its global organization was a matter of a dividing up of the world between powerful nations, which took place at summits such as the Berlin conference in 1885, where Africa was cut up like a cake, with this part given to France, this for England, this for Germany, and so on. A metropolitan power for the direct management of these territories was established, naturally along with the presence of large companies on the lookout for raw materials, and the complicity of certain important local figures.

And then there were the world wars, there were the wars of national liberation, there was the existence of the socialist bloc supporting the wars of national liberation. And in short, over the course of the 1960s and 1970s, all of that progressively put an end to this regime of direct administration that we called colonialism in the strict sense – that is to say, the installation of a metropolitan power in the dominated regions.

Despite all of this, the sovereign tasks of the protection of companies and the control of circuits of raw materials or energy sources were still pressing, and were taken on in part by statist means. They could not be entrusted to the mercenaries of private companies alone. Thus, for years, decades even, there was incessant military activity on the part of Western states. Remember that, just taking France's military interventions in Africa over the last forty years, there were more than fifty such episodes! We might say that France was in an almost chronic state of military mobilization in order to maintain its African turf. . . . And there were, as we know, great expeditions, gigantic conflicts, the Algerian War, the Vietnam War, and finally the destruction of Iraq, and then what is happening today.

So the point is not the end of imperial interventions, absolutely not. The question is one of different modes of imperial intervention. The question still remains: What to do in order to protect our interests in distant countries? On the question of the intervention in Mali, I read in a very serious journal that this intervention had been a success, because we had succeeded in 'protecting the interests of the West'. It was said just like that, in all innocence. So, in Mali, we protect the interests of the West. . . . We don't first of all protect the Malians, apparently. What is more, we cut their country in half. Defence of the West demands as much. So even if the modes of intervention have changed, the necessity of imperial interventions remains pressing, given the dimensions of the capitalist interests in play: uranium, petrol, diamonds, precious woods, rare metals, cocoa, coffee, bananas, gold, carbon, aluminium, gas. . . .

I think that what is coming into view is the idea that, rather than taking control of the arduous task of establishing states under the supervision of the metropolis, or further still, of directly metropolitan states, the possibility is that we simply *destroy states*. And you can see how consistent this possibility is with the progressive destatization of globalized capitalism. In certain geographical spaces full of dormant wealth, we can create free, anarchic zones where there is no longer any state, and where, consequently, we no longer have to enter into communication with that redoubtable monster that the state always is, even when it is weak. We can shield ourselves from the permanent risk that a state may prefer another client, and other commercial snags. In a zone where all true state power has gone, the whole petty world of firms can operate without any overall control. There will be a sort of semi-anarchy, with armed gangs, maybe controlled, maybe uncontrollable – but business can continue as usual, or even better than before. Even so, we must realize that, contrary to what is often said, contrary to what we are told, companies, their representatives, the general agents of capital, can perfectly well negotiate with armed gangs, and in certain ways can negotiate with them more easily than with established states. It is not true that stateless anarchy and the unimaginable cruelty that goes along with it necessarily stand in formal contradiction to the structure of the world as it is today. Everyone can see that we've been talking for quite some time now about crushing Daesh but that, in reality, so far, nothing really serious has been done, except by the Kurds, who are there on the ground and have their own interests in the region. Everyone says: 'Oh dear, send three thousand men over there? Maybe we should just carry on trying to more or less contain it, reduce it to a normal regime for doing business. . .'. After all, Daesh is a commercial power, a competent and multi-faceted commercial enterprise! It sells petrol, it sells works of art, it sells a lot of cotton, it is a major power in cotton production. It sells many things to everyone – because to sell something, there must be two. It's not Daesh who is buying Daesh's cotton.

To designate these new practices of imperialism, namely destroying states rather than corrupting or replacing them, I have proposed the word 'zoning'. I have suggested that the imperialism that arbitrarily fabricated cut-up pseudo-countries, countries under the supervision of the metropolis, has now been replaced, in Africa, in the Middle East, and in certain regions of Asia, by infra-state zones which in reality are areas of non-state pillaging. In these zones, we must no doubt intervene militarily from time to time, but without truly having responsibility for the whole laborious management of colonial states, nor even needing to keep in place, through corruption, a whole clique of local accomplices who take advantage of the functions granted them to pillage resources.

Let's recapitulate. We have a contemporary world structure dominated by the triumph of globalized capitalism. We have a strategic weakening of states, and even an ongoing process of the capitalist withering away of states. And thirdly, we have new practices of imperialism that tolerate, and in certain circumstances even encourage, the butchering and the annihilation of states.

This is not a negligible hypothesis if we ask, for example, what was the real interest of the expedition into Libya. A state was completely destroyed, a zone of anarchy was created that everyone complains about, or pretends to, but after all the Americans did the same thing in

Iraq, and the French before them in Mali and the Central African Republic. It even seems to me that the complete destruction of Yugoslavia, for which heavy Western interventions were necessary, already signalled the practices of zoning. Across substantial zones, the practice was to destroy states only to replace them with almost nothing – that is to say, nothing but fragile agreements between minorities, religious groups, and various armed gangs. We replaced the Sunnis with the Shiites, or vice versa, but all of this amounted to operations that were, in the serious sense of the term, non-state operations. It's quite obvious. But this had disastrous effects on the populations concerned, which we must now examine.

II

Effects on Populations

The first striking effect of everything I have set out here is that unequal development is at unprecedented levels. Even the parliamentary right wing are sometimes worried by it. There are inequalities so monstrous that, given the weakening of states, we no longer know how to control their effects on the life of populations.

On this point there are some fundamental figures that everyone should know, that everyone should have at hand, figures that underlie what we must indeed call a class logic – an extremely strict, extremely trenchant one which renders even the most formal democratic norm fatuous and impracticable. At a certain degree of inequality, to speak of democracy or of the democratic norm no longer makes any sense at all.

Let me remind you of these figures:

- 1% of the global population possess 46% of the available resources. 1% – 46%: that's almost half.
- 10% of the global population possess 86% of the available resources.
- 50% of the global population possess nothing.

Thus, the objective description of this situation, in terms of population, in terms of masses, tells us that we have a planetary oligarchy represented by around ten per cent of the population. This oligarchy, I repeat, owns 86 per cent of the available resources. Ten per cent of the population – not so far from the aristocracy of the *ancien régime*. It's pretty much of the same order. Our world reinstates, reconfigures, an oligarchical situation that it has passed through before, which was in place a long time ago and to which it is now returning in a new form.

So, we have an oligarchy of ten per cent, and then we have a destitute mass of almost half of the global population, the mass of the destitute population, the overwhelming majority of the African and Asian masses. The total now comes to around 60 per cent, and there remain the other 40 per cent. These 40 per cent are the middle classes. The middle classes who, laboriously, share out between them the remaining 14 per cent of the world's resources.

This is a very significant vision of the structure of the world: we have a mass of destitute people who make up half of the global population, we have an oligarchy whom I could well call aristocratic, from the point of view of their number. And then we have the middle classes, that pillar of democracy, who, representing 40 per cent of the population, must share between them 14 per cent of global resources.

This middle class is largely concentrated in the so-called advanced countries. So it is largely a Western class. It is the mass support for local democratic power, parliamentary power. I think that we can say, without wanting to insult its existence – since we're all more or less a part of it, aren't we? – that a very important aim of this group, which, even so, only has access to quite a small part of global resources, just 14 per cent, is not to fall back into, not to be identified with, the immense mass of the destitute. Which we can well understand.

This is why this class, taken as a whole, is porous to racism, to xenophobia, to hatred of the destitute. These are the subjective determinations that threaten this median mass which defines the West in the broad sense, or at least the representation it has of itself; and they are determinations that fuel a sentiment of superiority. We know very well that the Western middle class is the vector of the conviction that the West, in the end, is the place of the civilized.

When we read everywhere that we must wage war on the barbarians, it is obviously being said in the name of the civilized, and in so far as these barbarians come from the enormous mass of those who are left behind, and with whom the middle class does not want to identify, at any cost.

All of this clarifies the singular position of the middle class, especially the European middle class. It is like a photographic plate sensitive to the difference – which is constantly threatened by the capitalist real – between itself, the middle class, and the enormous mass, far away, somewhat distant, but which also has its representatives in our own countries, of those who have little or nothing. And it is to this middle class threatened by precarity that we owe the discourse of the defence of values: 'We must defend our values!' In reality, to defend our values means to defend the Western way of life, that is to say the civilized sharing-out of 14 per cent of global resources between 40 per cent of the 'median' population. Pascal Bruckner, head held high like Hollande in his role as war chief, tells us that this way of life is not negotiable. 'The Western way of life is not negotiable.' This according to Pascal Bruckner who, himself, in any case, will not negotiate. With anyone. He is already convinced, Bruckner is; he dons his uniform: War! War! Such is his wish, his catechism.

This is one of the reasons why the mass murder of which we speak this evening is significant and traumatizing. For it strikes within a Europe which, in certain regards, is the soft underbelly of globalized capitalism; it strikes at the heart of the middle mass, the middle class which represents itself as an island of civilization at the centre of a world – whether it is a matter of the oligarchy who are so few that we can hardly see them, or the immense mass of the destitute – that surrounds them, enframes them and presses close to them, this middle class. This is the reason why the sinister event was experienced as a crisis of civilization, that is to say as an attack on something which already, in its historical and natural existence, is threatened by developments underway in globalized capitalism, but to which we nevertheless cling.

This is the first effect of the structure of globalized capitalism on populations. But apart from this there is something else that is very important in understanding what has happened. In the world today there are a little over two billion people of whom we can say that they are counted for nothing. It is not even that they belong, as they obviously do, to the mass of the destitute 50 per cent. It's worse: they are counted for nothing *by capital*, meaning that from the point of view of the structural development of the world, they are nothing, and that therefore, strictly speaking, they should not exist. They should not be there. It would be better for them not to be there. But they are there all the same.

What does it mean to say that they are counted for nothing? It means that they are neither consumers nor a labour force. Because there are only two modes of existence for capital, if you don't belong to the oligarchy: you must be an employee, making a bit of money; and then you must spend this money by consuming products that are manufactured by the same capital. Your identity in the eyes of the dominant tendency of today's world is the double identity, structured by money, of employee and consumer.

Now, there are two billion adults who have no access to either of these identities. They have no access to work, nor are they students, or retired, and, by way of consequence, nor do they have access to the market. From the point of view of the general logic of the world, of imperious and self-satisfied capitalist globalization, they are as if non-existent. What is more, we are beginning to hear propaganda concerning the extremely dangerous threat of an invasion of our dear civilized Europe by these people who do not exist or should not exist. Everything concerning the question of migratory movements, or the question of the birth rate in Africa, is directly connected to this agonizing question: 'My God! Are we going to see a massive influx of these people into our country because their number is growing, even though there are already probably two billion of them?' Once we have got to that point, to go from the fact that they should not exist to practices that ensure their inexistence is only one more step.

But where does this mass of people come from, these people whose existence the contemporary world counts for nothing? To understand this point, it is enough to be a little bit – just a little bit – Marxist. Capital, and thus those who own it, only value the labour force – meaning that they only employ people in the companies they direct – because they can make a profit from doing so. This is what Marx called, in his jargon, the extraction of surplus value. So there is no necessary reason to think that capital is able to value *all* of the available labour force. There have already been other periods of mass unemployment, notably in the 1930s, after the great crisis of 1929. But today it seems that, even beyond the crisis that began in 2008, this impasse of employment is more structural, and even definitive. Globalization perhaps makes it intrinsically impossible for a capitalism that has achieved its maximal extension to value, in the form of the profits that can be made from them, the available labour force. And perhaps this is aggravated further: perhaps the system of profit, which is the unique source of the dynamic of capital, has hit a barrier created by its own extension where, in order to value all of the available labour force, average working hours would have to be lowered considerably, so as to be able to hire the two billion people who have been stranded.

Now, this can't happen. Why can't it happen? Because average working hours can't be lowered. And why not? Well, very simply because of the mechanisms of profit production: we know that a significant number of work hours are destined for the production of surplus-value and that, below this number, a profit will no longer be made. In all probability, to have a reasonable capitalist valuation of the labour force today, average working hours on a global scale would have to continue to be around forty hours per week. And during those hours there will be two billion people, and probably more, who have no work.

We could therefore calculate the other way around. We could say: taking account of the situation, a reasonable global government which cares about the public good might think it necessary to decide – as Marx imagined would take place – that average working hours on a global scale must be reduced to twenty hours. Perhaps less. Obviously this enormous mass of people who cannot find work would rapidly be absorbed – they would become employed. The decrease in working hours was a central point in Marx's reformist-revolutionary propositions, since he saw very well that, in order to wrest work away from the domination of capital, mass worker action would have to push for a decrease in working hours, to the point where capital would no longer be able to tolerate it.

But for the moment, it is capital that has won out. And since it is capital that has won, it does not tolerate a decrease in working hours, not even the meagre decrease to thirty-five hours proposed by Martine Aubry. And those who cannot find their place within this framework – well, it fearlessly declares that they are nothing. This is why in our world there is an enormous mass of people who are counted for nothing. This is a point that is absolutely necessary to take into account if we want to understand what has happened.

Let's note also the geography of all of this: the spatial distribution of this available labour force counted for nothing is clearly linked to zoning. In the zones where the situation is anarchic, where the state is absent, and where armed gangs circulate, one resigns oneself without much bother to the fact that the populations there will, strictly speaking, be without any established defence, and that they will rot away in 'humanitarian' camps. Why worry too much about their existence, since they are neither consumers nor a labour force? They will just have to make their way, between armed gangs and capitalist predators of every stripe, and do whatever they can to stay alive.

This explains why entire zones are given over to a fascist-type political gangsterism – which would not be the case, and could not be the case, were there not billions of people who are counted for nothing. If, through a rational system of working hours, everyone was integrated into the figures of ordinary sociality, of common sociality, these situations of banditry and human trafficking would be impossible. But the combination of zoning – that is, the destruction of states by Western predators – and the phenomenon of the existence of millions or billions of people who are counted for nothing, leads to the existence, across substantial swathes of the planet, sometimes entire, immense countries like the Congo, of what can be called a gangster-type domination.

What do we mean by this? Certain kinds of savage, armed capitalist firms occupy the spaces left empty where the state has disappeared, conscripting those who have been left abandoned, in particular children and adolescents, and indulge in pillaging which supplies the global market. As when Daesh sells columns of trucks carrying petrol to Turkey. It is in this context that fascist armed gangs with a religious tinge begin to appear.

Ah! Religion! Islam! At last you got there, our great Islamophobic thinkers will be saying. Yes, yes, I'm getting there. But I want to say at once that religion has always been available as a pretext, a rhetorical cover, manipulable and manipulated by fascist gangs. Christianity is no exception. Just take Spanish fascism, Franco's fascism, extremely keen on mass executions, even a long time after the end of the Civil War: this fascism was literally glued to the Catholic religion. Franco's armed gangs were blessed by priests, and one spoke of the great Catholic Spain that was going to replace the terrible republican Spain. Yet in reality it was just a question of state power and its sacking by the fascists. So it is hardly credible to lay the blame on Islam, frankly. Above all, the nature of these armed gangs is to occupy a devastated capitalist-type terrain in order to establish a profitable gangsterism, which subsequently, to appeal to young people in revolt, may take on the most various of spiritual aspects. Religions, just like other ideologies – including, alas, revolutionary ideologies – have always been susceptible to being combined with mafia-like practices. The Italian mafia themselves, the mafia of the godfathers, still profess a punctilious Catholicism.

But all of this relates to the subjective aspect of our situation.

III

Reactive Subjectivities

At this stage, I want to come to the typical sub-jectivities that appear in our conjuncture. By 'typical subjectivity' I understand the psychic forms, the forms of conviction and of affect, that are produced by the world of which I speak. This is not a catalogue of all possible subjectivities, but of those that I consider as being induced or produced by the structure of the contemporary world.

I think there are three: Western subjectivity, the subjectivity of desire for the West – which is not the same thing – and the subjectivity that I would call 'nihilist'. I think that these three subjectivities are the typical creations of the contemporary state of the world.

Western subjectivity is the subjectivity of those who share the 14 per cent left over by the dominant oligarchy. It is the subjectivity of the middle class, and it is largely concentrated in the most developed countries. It is here that the crumbs can be shared out. This subjectivity, as we see it functioning today, is in my view beset by a contradiction. Its first element is a great self-satisfaction – Westerners are very happy with themselves, they like themselves a lot. There is a historical arrogance behind this, of course: it was not so long ago that Westerners held the world in their hands. At that time, one needed only to add up the possessions of the French and the English, obtained by pure violence, and one would have practically the whole map of the extra-European world. What remains of this direct and immense imperial power is a self-image of the Westerner as, in some way, the representative of the modern world, as having invented the modern way of life and being its defender.

But this is just one side of things. The other side is a constant fear. The constant fear of what? I would say, employing a rather brutal materialism, the fear of sliding from the side of the shared 14 per cent onto the side of the 50 per cent who have nothing. In the world such as it is, members of the middle class are what one might call a privileged few. And the constant fear of a privileged few is that they might lose their privilege.

For it may be, given the tensions of contemporary capitalism, that a middle class will no longer be able to exist as before. This is not impossible. It's not impossible, given the increasing rapacity of the oligarchy and the costly conflicts that it is bound to pursue in order to defend its profit zones, that the middle class will no longer be allowed its 14 per cent of available resources, but only 12 per cent, for example. And then we'll see the looming spectre of what has been called the 'pauperization of the middle classes'.

This is why we have a typically Western dialectical relation between an extreme arrogant self-satisfaction and a constant fear. Whence the definition of the art of democratic government these days: it is the art of making sure that this fear which animates their ideological and electoral base, the middle class, is not directed against them – the governments – but against this or that representative of the destitute masses. This is a major operation: to convince the middle classes that there are indeed risks; that their fear is legitimate; and that this fear is not at all motivated by the wise measures put in place by the government and by the democratic management of business, but that its unique cause is the intolerable pressure constantly exerted on the middle classes by the enormous destitute masses, and in particular by its representatives inside our societies: foreign workers, their children, refugees, the inhabitants of dark cities, fanatical Muslims. Here is the scapegoat sent out to pasture, by our masters and their media hacks, to feed on the fear of the middle classes; the organization of a sort of rampant civil war whose sinister effects we are seeing more and more of. Such are the subjective vicissitudes of those who, in a certain sense, represent the very body of the West.

Now consider those who are neither of the oligarchy nor of the middle class. That is to say, those who are neither consumers nor employees, and who therefore are situated outside of the world market. It must be understood that they are constantly exposed to the spectacle of the luxury and arrogance of these first two groups. The mass media purveys it, and the mass media goes everywhere the global expansion of capitalism goes, organizing the permanent spectacle of this expansion. Here we have two absolutely linked phenomena. And what is more, the planetary media are concentrated in gigantic multinational firms such as Apple, Google, and so on.

The effect of this spectacular accompaniment is that not only is the Western way of life, the dominant way of life, non-negotiable, as the valorous Bruckner says, but that, what's more, it is shown to the whole world as such. And so the destitute, wherever they may be, enjoy the constant spectacle of the luxury and arrogance of the others. And this (although hopefully not definitively) without giving rise to any overall ideological and political movement that would aim to counteract, and then do away with, the hegemony of capitalism. These destitute masses see that there is somewhere a nucleus of luxury, of arrogance, of pretension to civilization, to modernity, which they do not have the means to really oppose in thought or in action, any more than they share in its reality. And the result is a bitter frustration, a classic mixture of envy and revolt.

Whence the other two typical subjectivities. The one that comes first is what I call desire for the West: the desire to possess, to share in what is represented, what is vaunted everywhere as the

48

luxury of the West. Thus one adopts middle-class behaviour and habits of consumption without having the means to do so. This obviously gives rise to phenomena such as migratory flows, for the elementary form of desire for the West is quite simply the desire to leave the devastated zones to join this famous Western world, since life is so good there, since everyone is happy and bathes in magnificent modern luxury. And if one cannot go there, then one can indulge in local alienations – that is to say, the tendency to copy, with impoverished means, the configurations of Western modes of life. One might speak at length on this theme of desire for the West, which is fundamental today in the world and which has considerable effects, all disastrous.

The last subjectivity, nihilist subjectivity, is a desire for revenge and destruction, which obviously is coupled with the desire for departure and alienated imitation. It is natural that this violent desire for revenge and destruction is often expressed, formalized, in reactive mythologies, in the exaltation of traditionalisms that one claims to be defending, possibly by force of arms, against the Western way of life, against desire for the West.

Here, it is a question of the nihilism of he whose life is counted for nothing. This nihilism is seemingly constituted against the desire for the West, but only because desire for the West is its hidden shadow. If the nihilist did not activate the death drive, if he did not give free reign to his aggression, and ultimately to murderous aggression, he knows very well that in reality he too would succumb to the desire for the West, which is already present in him.

We must see clearly that these two typical subjectivities – the subjectivity of desire for the West and the nihilist subjectivity of revenge and destruction – form a couplet that gravitates, like a positive and negative version, around the fascination exerted by Western domination.

And all of this in a context where there is no proposal for any sort of collective uprising that would affirm and organize the perspective of another structuring of the world. Meaning that these three typical subjectivities are really entirely internal to the structure of the world as I have described it. And it is on the basis of this interiority that I will characterize what I call contemporary fascism.

IV

Contemporary Fascism

Generally speaking, I think that we can call 'fascism' the popular subjectivity that is generated and triggered by capitalism either when there is a grave systemic crisis – as was the case in the 1930s – or, perhaps more profoundly, under the effects of the structural limits of capitalism brought to light by its globalization – a globalization which, let us recall, is at once an expansion and the revelation of its incapacity to value the whole of the available labour force.

Fascism is a reactive subjectivity. It is intra-capitalist, since it proposes no other structure of the world, and it is embedded in the world market, in so far as it reproaches capitalism for not being able to keep the promises that it makes.

In turning to fascism, the disappointment of the desire for the West becomes the enemy of the West, because in reality its desire for the West is not satisfied. This fascism forms an aggressive, nihilist and destructive drive because it is constituted on the basis of an intimate and negative repression of desire for the West. It is largely a repressed desire for the West, whose place is taken up by a deadly nihilist reaction whose target is precisely that which was the possible object of desire. A classic psychoanalytical schema, then.

As for its form, we can define modern fascism as a death drive articulated in a language of identity. It is entirely possible for religion to be an ingredient in this articulation: Catholicism played this role for Spanish fascism during the Civil War, Islam is playing it today for the Middle East, particularly where imperial zoning has destroyed states. But religion is just a cover, it is not at all what is at the bottom of all this, it is a form of subjectivation but not the real content of the thing. The real content to which the debris of the religious fable lends its identitarian representation derives from the omnipresence of the desire for the West, whether in its affirmed and explicit form or in its deadly repressed form.

The practical form of these fascisms is always the logic of the gang, criminal gangsterism, with the conquest and defence of territories or business monopolies, just like the dealer in his 'hood'. To keep a grip on things, one needs the spectacular character of cruelty, pillage and then, in the case of other mafias, the permanent recycling of goods in the global market. Just as nihilist desire is only the flipside of desire for the West, so the destatized zones where nihilist subjectivity prospers are articulated with the global market, and thus with the reality of the West. Daesh, as I have said, is a commercial company selling petrol, artworks, cotton, arms and many other things. And its mercenaries are in fact employees, with certain extra privileges, owing to their pillaging and their reduction of captives to slavery.

In reality, then, this fascizing form is internal to the globalized capitalist structure, of which it is in a certain sense a subjective perversion. What's more, everyone knows that companies, and also confirmed Western clients such as the Saudi government, are continually negotiating with fascist gangs installed in the Middle East zones, and that they negotiate their own interests as best they can. Let us say finally that this fascism is the obverse of a frustrated desire for the West, organized more or less militarily on the flexible model of the mafia gang, and with various ideological colourings in which religion plays a purely formal part.

What interests me here is what this fascizing subjectivity offers to the young. After all, the killers of January 2016, like those of November, were young people, young people from France. They are young men between twenty and thirty years old, largely from an immigrant worker background, second or third generation. These youths consider themselves as being without prospects, without any place in society they could occupy. Even those who are educated to some extent, who have a baccalaureate, have no vision for themselves: there is no place for them; at least no place that conforms to their desire. These youths therefore see themselves as being on the margins of the salaried class, of consumption, and of the future. So what fascization offers to them (what is stupidly called 'radicalization', when in fact it is a pure and simple regression) is a mixture of sacrificial and criminal heroism and 'Western' satisfactions. On the one hand, the youth will become something like a mafioso, and proud of it, capable of sacrificial and criminal heroism: kill the Westerners, wipe out the killers of other gangs, indulge in spectacular cruelty, take over territories, and so on. This, on the one hand; and then, on the other, touches of the 'good life', various satisfactions. Daesh pays its group of thugs rather well, much better than they would 'normally' get in the zones where they live. They have a little money, they have women, they have cars, and all the rest. So it's a mixture of deadly heroic propositions and, at the same time, Western corruption by products. And this is a consistent mixture that has always, fundamentally, been characteristic of fascist gangs.

Religion can perfectly well act as an identitarian sauce for all of this, precisely in so far as it is a suitably anti-Western referent. But as we have seen, in the final analysis, the origin of these youths doesn't matter much, their spiritual origin, their religious origin, and so on, as they say. What counts is the choice they have made about their frustration. And they will rally to this mixture of corruption and sacrificial and criminal heroism because of the subjectivity that is theirs, not because of their Islamic conviction.

What is more, we have seen that in most cases Islamization is terminal rather than inaugural. Let's say that it's fascization that Islamizes, not Islam that fascizes.

V

Who Are the Killers?

Given these conditions, who are the November killers, and what can we say of their acts? Let's say that the killers are young fascists, in the sense I just described. A comparison I would willingly make is between them and certain of the fascizing *miliciens* in France during the last war. In these bands of young *miliciens*, collaborators with the Germans, there was also an aspect of 'Viva la muerte!', a certain note of: 'we can do what we like, we're armed, we can kill, we can torture'. There was an openly advertised cruelty. And then there were also a whole heap of petty profits – the good life, barcrawls, nice cars, cash, girls. . . . So it was a mixture of the same ingredients. And, in a sense, for the same reasons. What were they, these *miliciens*? They were French, but the French of a civil war, acting against the most self-evident national interests, since they collaborated with the Nazi occupiers. There was something conflicted in this. Like their imam, Pétain, they abundantly saluted France, with the national flag – 'La France! La France!' – even while they worked, in the most sordid conditions, against the most elementary national interests, the perennial interests of not being occupied by a foreign power. This is what I call an internal scission within this fascist subjectivity. The killers of today are, in a certain sense, typical products of frustrated desire for the West, people inhabited by a repressed desire, constituted by this desire. They imagine that they are driven by anti-Western passion, but they are only one of the nihilist symptoms of the blind emptiness of globalized capitalism, of its inability to count everyone in the world that it has shaped.

Their act – a blind mass murder – is not an attack. An attack is something organized by the Resistance against the Nazi occupiers and their Pétainist accomplices, or better still, the attack that the glorious Russian populists mounted to kill the Tsar. In fact, if we look at how the massacre of Friday 13 November played out, it was neither an organized affair nor a military attack; ultimately, it was a bloody attack but a bungled operation. That didn't matter, though, since the young fascists had decided that their life did not count. This is the absolute wellspring of this kind of affair. Their own life did not count. And since their own lives did not count, the lives of others meant nothing to them either. It is truly nihilism that is at the bottom of this murderousness. In the end one is going to burn out one's life in a 'heroism' as ridiculous and artificial as it is criminal. I think that we should call it a horrific 'mass murder' in which, just as horrific, the murderer has included himself. Here we have a suicidal form of crime that takes the death drive to its lowest point. Nothing is left, neither victims nor assassins.

As we can see, it is an atrocious and criminal fascist act. However, is it enough to speak of 'barbarians', as has become the official appellation? This word 'barbarian' has always been opposed to the 'civilized'. The 'war on the barbarians' is the war of the civilized against the barbarians. But there is no reason to concede to Western arrogance that it represents civilization in the face of such an atrocious criminal act. This is the moment to recall that today Western killing is a permanent and extraordinarily bloody fact.

There are just three examples:

(1) Westerners now have the power, with drones, but also with teams specializing in what in France are called 'homo' (for 'homicide') missions, to assassinate people on the secret orders of heads of state. Murder is more convenient with drones, for one no longer even needs to leave the office. Neither Obama nor Hollande scorns these means, the convenient and the less convenient alike. But in the case of drones, there are recorded statistics: for a highly targeted death (say, a gang chief), there are on average nine collateral victims, who could be anyone, children from the neighbourhood perhaps. That's drones for you. So, if you multiply the targeted drone assassinations that Obama has calmly carried out during his term of office, you very quickly end up with hundreds and hundreds of people who have been massacred for nothing. If we call killing people for nothing 'barbarian', then the West are barbarous every day, and

we should realize this. Quite simply, in the first case of barbarianism, the barbarianism of the barbarians, we have a deliberate and suicidal mass murder. In the case of the barbarianism of the civilized, it is a technological mass murder, dissimulated and self-satisfied.

(2) The proportion of Western deaths in explicitly declared wars, such as Iraq or Palestine, is around one in twenty. The West have gone so far as to claim that the aim is zero deaths on their side and all deaths on the other side, which is a very particular mode of warfare. They haven't quite got there yet. But nearly, if we count the deaths in the Iraq, Afghan, Palestinian and other conflicts, which average one death on one side against twenty on the other. And people notice this fantastic disproportionality: those who live in this type of situation see very well that this is how it works; and for them, the greatest barbarian is the West.

(3) Even without going into its political significance, look at the case of Gaza: 2,000 Palestinian deaths, including 450 children. So this is civilized? Just because it was aeroplanes that killed, shredded, crushed, and burned

people, and not young idiots who opened fire into the crowd before killing themselves?

The killers are young fascists who are like Pétain's *miliciens*, and whose motives are confused, deadly, and, what's more, without any real content. But there is no particular reason to act as if, as opposed to these people, the Western armies represent civilization. It's something that just isn't admissible. War is war, it is always more or less murky slaughter, and we ourselves have tortured, killed, deported just as many, and more, in the colonial wars, and since then. And we will continue to do so on a grand scale, if, as our governments proclaim, the time has come for a final war on 'terrorism'.

VI

The State's Reaction: 'France' and 'War'

I think that the fundamental function of a state such as the French state is to discipline the middle classes. And to a spectacular degree, this is the work of the Left. The Left is excellent when it comes to disciplining the middle classes. During my youth, during the Algerian war, it was the Left, who, with Guy Mollet, were in charge of the government that obtained 'special powers' to launch a total war. It does indeed seem that, in order to discipline the middle classes by saying to them 'war, war' – when war hardly belongs to the habits of the aforementioned class – what is really needed is the authority of an arrant socialist.

So obviously this disciplining of the middle classes under the slogan of war is also a fiction.

It's a deception; no one is ready to go to war here, in this country. The word 'war' is not in its place. In January the state used republican laicity, this time it tries to use good old nationalism, France, the tricolour flag coupled with what is their perennial trump card, 'it's war'. But today, this coupling is obviously aberrant. And what is more, in my view, it will not work for long.

So I want to say a few words about these two words.

Let's start with 'France'. France, today, is a signifier with no definable positive content. What is 'France' today? It is a second-class actor within the world structure that I have described. And then we say 'our values!', but what are the values of France? I have my own point of view on this. France, what is singular about France – because if there are French values, we must ask what is singular about them – is the revolutionary tradition. Republican first of all, from the 1789 revolution. And then socialist, anarcho-syndicalist, communist, and finally leftist – all of this between 1789 and, let's say, 1976.

But all that's over. It's over. France can no longer be represented today in any credible way as being the privileged site of a revolutionary tradition. Rather, it is characterized by a singular collection of identitarian intellectuals. This is also manifested by something that has never happened anywhere else: openly discriminatory laws concerning a part of the poor that it has created. The laws about the wearing of the Islamic veil, these are terrible – laws of stigmatization and segregation – targeting whom? Targeting the poor, the poor populations who have their religion, just in the way that the Breton domestics and workers were Catholic in times past. Demonizing them, when it is French capitalism that has created their poverty. Why? Because it is capitalism that destroyed French industry. Why did so many people come from the Third World to France? Because we went to get them! We must remember the period from the 1950s to the 1980s when we flew to Morocco to find workers who were needed for work on factory production lines. These people brought their families, there was a second generation, there were youths who expected to become workers, qualified workers, technicians. . . . But we destroyed the apparatus of production, the factories are almost gone, everything is increasingly outsourced. So these youths have no future. But all of this is founded on a deception, a detestable fraud. We imported them with no guarantee, and now we want to export them again. . . . But you can't do that; you don't treat 'human material' like that, surely? . . . So I really think that today 'France' means all of that, and it doesn't add up to any significant, visible, or interesting emblem. And those who are having identitarian jitters over France, we can see very well what they want. Ultimately, as is always the case, they want us to persecute the others. Because ultimately that is what identity always is, in the final analysis, if it is not of universal significance as in the revolutionary tradition. An identity that does not have a universal signification can only be defined by persecution of those who do not fall under it. There is no other way to give it a semblance of life. Those who say 'France, France', what are they doing for France? Well, they bellow against the Arabs, that's pretty much it. And I don't see that as an eminent service rendered to France. It doesn't particularly honour the French. Meanwhile, fewer than three per cent of these courageous 'French' would be prepared to die for their country.

As for war, one thing is clear: it is not 'barbarians' who have declared war; it is the French state that, in the wake of private firms and some-times the Americans, has gone to mix itself up in murky imperial affairs, to participate in zoning, to destroy states, and which in doing so has cre-ated the whole situation whose panorama I've tried to paint here. And this situation includes the subjective genesis of young fascists in the zones devastated of any social life, and the fact that a whole segment of the global population is counted for nothing.

VII

The Conditions of a Return to a Politics of Emancipation, Detached from the Schema of the Contemporary World

I am coming to the point that will bring this all to a conclusion: How, in these conditions, can we try to construct a different way of thinking? How can we tear ourselves away from all of this? I mean to say: tear ourselves away from the propaganda that accompanies every declaration of war, even if this 'war' is fictional, fraudulent. There is a great tradition of declarations of war, nationalist rants, and absolutely fictional propaganda. You only have to look at the literature concerning the 'Boche' in 1914. Monsters! Assassins! But in truth, we must say, the Boche in 1914 were not so different from the French.

So, what is to be done? I think firstly that, as far as the space defined as 'France' and the phantoms of the 'French' are concerned, we should replace them, mentally and practically, with an international space. A way of thinking internationally, I would even say transnationally, that would be able to measure up to capitalist globalization. Because the capitalists stopped being French a long, long time ago; they have a head start on us. They are at home in Shanghai, they are at home in San Francisco, in Morocco, in the Congo, in Sao Paolo. . . .

And, as for us, we want to be little middle-class French huddled together in France? How utterly behind the times. And all the more so if we aggravate this backward-looking attitude with our inability to recognize as being with us, and of us, the people who are here, on the ridiculous pretext that they're Muslims, or that they come from Africa, or, worse still, that they dress like this and not like that, or that they eat meat prepared in a particular way! If, in our turn, we count for nothing, or even as enemies, people who live here but who, for capital, count as nothing. If we are incapable of speaking with and acting with these people – especially with them – so as to create an opening in the situation, a new political path. If we are unable to undertake with them our affirmative, creative exit from a benighted West. . . .

It is terrible to consider that the revolutionary defeat has been such that we are not even in a position to be able to put together a globalized mental representation of the problems, whereas our immediate adversaries mastered this a long time ago. And they mastered it precisely to the detriment of everything that the protection of states had to offer. In turn, we must find the force to partially disinterest ourselves in the state itself, or at least in the state as it is. Stop voting! Don't lend any importance to the lying, vain proclamations of our governments! Let's go elsewhere, to the places where, sometimes indistinct but always real, the popular will is alive. Because the state is what comes along when 'France' no longer means much. It is then that the state calls us, as it does today. But we know that the state, in every way, is at this moment nothing but an agent of the new globalized spread of capital.

There is certainly a contradiction between the fascist and criminal destination of frustration on one hand, and the global development of capitalism and its mass support, the middle class, on the other. There is a deadly contradiction, we can see this very well. However, it is a subjective contradiction internal to capitalism itself. It is not a contradiction between Good and Evil. It is not a contradiction between the values of Civilization and Barbarianism. It is a kind of internal torsion in which the West comes under attack from a part of its own impotence – its impotence when it comes to creating a habitable subjective space for all the youth of the world.

This excuses nothing; it excuses no crime. Fascism in all its forms is horrific. But we must understand this contradiction, the contradiction between the deadly nihilism of fascists and the destructive and empty imperial deployment of globalized capitalism, of which we cannot and must not become the agents. In none of our most essential determinations can we allow ourselves to be structured by this contradiction.

What we are suffering from is the absence, on the global scale, of a politics that would be detached entirely from the interiority of capitalism. It is the absence on the global scale of this politics that causes a young fascist to appear, to be created. It is not the young fascist, banditry, and religion, that create the absence of a politics of emancipation able to construct its own vision and to define its own practices. It is the absence of this politics that creates the possibility of fascism, of banditry, and of religious hallucinations.

I think now of the tragedy of Phaedra, in Racine's play, when Phaedra says, at the moment when she must declare her love, which to her own eyes is a criminal love: 'My wound is not so recent.' We, also, can say that our wound is not so recent as immigration, as Islam, as the devastation of the Middle East, as Africa being subjected to pillaging . . . our wound comes from the historical defeat of communism. Indeed, it is not so recent.

By 'communism' I understand simply the name, the historical name, given to a strategic thought detached from the hegemonic structure of capitalism. Its fate was probably sealed in the middle of the 1970s. And it is because of this that the periodization that I propose starts with the 1980s, when we began to feel the deleterious effects of this failure, in the form of a new energy of capitalism.

Where are we today? There are local experiments, there are convictions, we cannot say that there is nothing. There is a whole series of things that need to be irrigated by a new thinking.

And there is also a very clear representation of the forces at our disposal. There is a nomadic proletariat that comes from the most devastated zones. This nomad proletariat is very strongly internationalized already, and spread across the whole earth. Many workers in Korea are Nepalese, or come from Bangladesh, just as a whole mass of workers here have come from Morocco or Mali. . . . There is this enormous nomadic proletariat, which constitutes a virtual advance guard of the gigantic mass of people whose existence, in the world today, is not counted.

And then there are also intellectuals, middle-class people, Western ones included, who are available for this new thinking – who uphold it, or try to do so. The whole problem lies in their connecting themselves with this nomad proletariat, going to see them, talking to them. No new thinking in politics will be born except through unexpected, improbable alliances, egalitarian trajectories and encounters.

And then there is the youth. . . . There is a youth who, for the reasons I have mentioned, when it arrives on the threshold of the world, asks what the world has in store for it. And perhaps it doesn't want to embed itself in one of the three figures I've called typical. Perhaps it doesn't want to intone the song of the glory of the West; perhaps it doesn't want to be driven by a desire for that glory or to invest its destiny in it; but perhaps it also doesn't want to invest its destiny in a murderous nihilism. But so long as no other proposition is made to it, it will remain essentially disoriented. Capitalism is a machine for disorienting subjects, if they don't resign themselves to simply inhabiting the vacuous duality consumer/employee.

And if this proposition is made, if there is an irrigation by this new thought, this will be what will overcome contemporary fascism – not the sordid wars of the state, which promise us nothing good. It will be the capacity to absorb and to annul rampant fascization, because there will be something else on the table. We will create a fourth typical subjective figure, one that seeks to go beyond the domination of globalized capitalism without falling into nihilism, that murderous avatar of desire for the West. This is what is essential. And in order for this to take place, peculiar alliances must be forged; we must think on another scale. Intellectuals, and different segments of youth, must become organically linked, by experiments at first local, and then wider – the scale of these things doesn't matter so much, given where we are right now. What matters is that youths of every provenance, and intellectuals, make a gesture, carve out a path, make a step towards the nomad proletariat.

There is an urgency here, but it is a strategic urgency that concerns everyone. It is a task, a task for us all. It is a work of thought, but it is also the work, the path, of going to see who is this other of whom you speak, who he really is, to gather his thoughts, his ideas, his vision of things; and for you to inscribe him – him, and you yourself at the same time – within a strategic vision of the destiny of humanity that will try to change the direction of the oblique history of humanity, try to make humanity tear itself away from the opaque misfortune into which, at the moment, it has sunk.

I am an incurable optimist, am I not? So I think that this is what will be done. But time is running out. Time is running out. . . .